mitten/kitten

By Jerome Martin

A TRUMPET CLUB SPECIAL EDITION

m

kitten

m

donkey

j

fudge

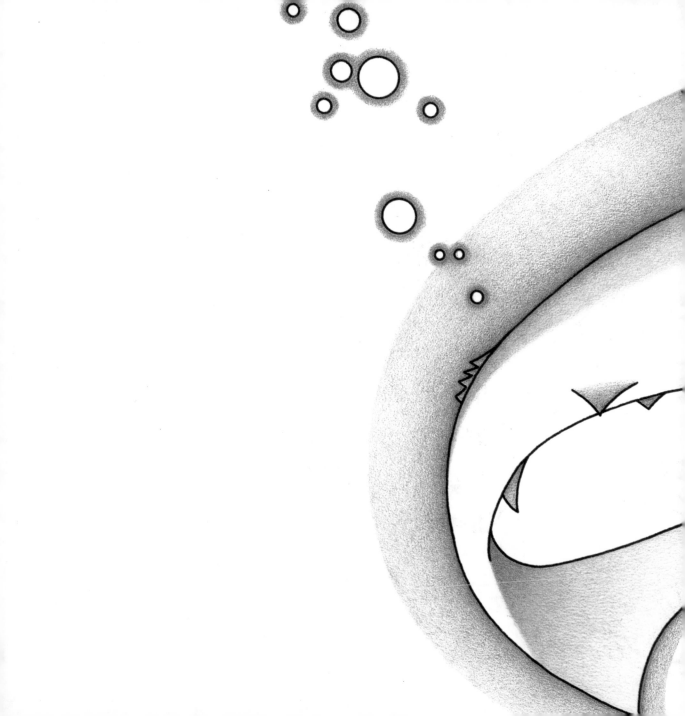

sh

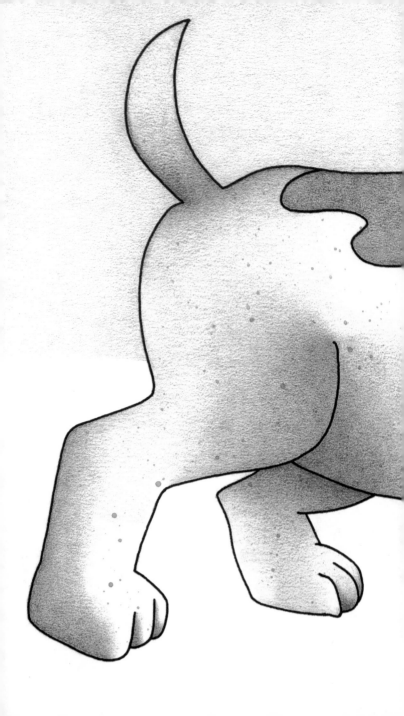

cr

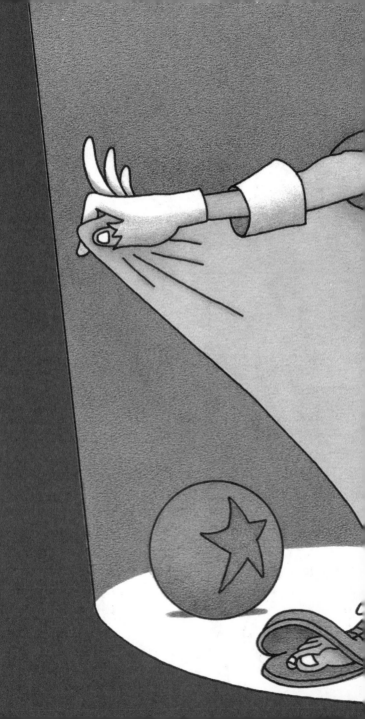

clown

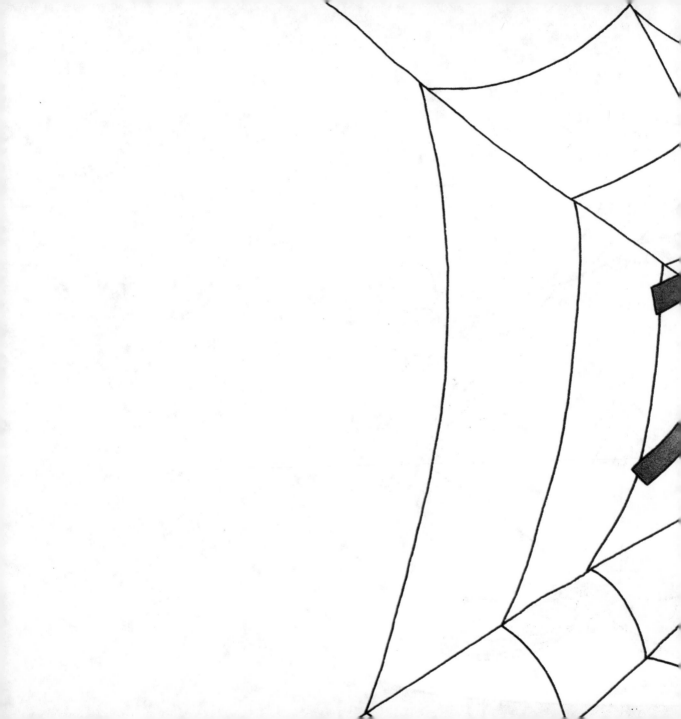

sp

rider

f

stork

cr

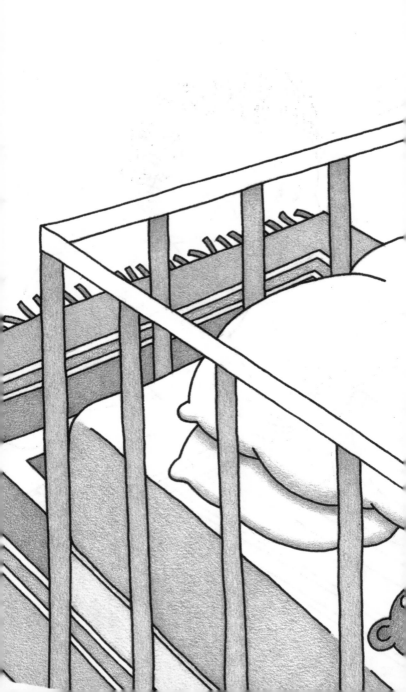

Published by The Trumpet Club
666 Fifth Avenue, New York, New York 10103

Copyright © 1991 by Jerome Martin

ISBN 0-440-84522-X

This edition published by arrangement with
Simon and Schuster Books for Young Readers,
a division of Simon & Schuster, Inc.

Designed by Vicki Kalajian

Note: The concept, text and illustrations for
Mitten/Kitten are the work of Jerome Martin.
With the author's permission, the illustrations
for this edition have been redone by Daniel Collins
based on Jerome Martin's originals.

Printed in the United States of America
November 1991

10 9 8 7 6 5 4 3 2 1

sleep

mitten/kitten

sleep

mitten/kitten

Published by The Trumpet Club
666 Fifth Avenue, New York, New York 10103

ISBN 0-440-84522-X

This edition published by arrangement with
Simon and Schuster Books for Young Readers,
a division of Simon & Schuster, Inc.

Designed by Vicki Kalajian

Note: The concept, text and illustrations for
Mitten/Kitten are the work of Jerome Martin.
With the author's permission, the illustrations
for this edition have been redone by Daniel Collins
based on Jerome Martin's originals.

Printed in the United States of America
November 1991

10 9 8 7 6 5 4 3 2 1